Getting To Know...

Nature's Children

PENGUINS

Merebeth Switzer

SCHOLASTIC INC.

New York Toronto London Auckland Sydney
Mexico City New Delhi Hong Kong Buenos Aires

Facts in Brief

Classification of the penguin

      Class: *Aves* (birds)

      Order: *Sphenisciformes* (penguins)

      Family: *Spheniscidae* (penguin family)

      Genus: There are six genera of penguins.

      Species: There are eighteen species of penguins.

World distribution. Penguins are found only in the seas of the Southern Hemisphere.

Habitat. Ocean and rocky coasts.

Distinctive physical characteristics. Penguins are flightless birds adapted for life in the ocean with webbed feet and small flipper-like wings.

Habits. Lay and hatch eggs in large groups; males and females share in the raising of the young.

Diet. Fish, crustaceans and small squids.

Published by Scholastic Inc.
90 Old Sherman Turnpike, Danbury, Connecticut 06816.

SCHOLASTIC and associated logos are trademarks of Scholastic Inc.

ISBN 0-7172-6687-7   Printed in the U.S.A.

Have you ever wondered . . .

Two black and white shapes zip through the water, plunging and diving at incredible speeds. At first, they appear to be fish. But look closer and you will see that they are penguins.

Penguins are amazingly agile. Sometimes they swim towards each other so quickly you expect them to crash. Then, at the last moment, *swoosh!* Without any warning they somersault, turn and streak away. These black and white daredevil birds are perfectly at home "flying" through the ocean. Turn the page to find out more about these underwater acrobats.

Penguins do not fly through the air,
but they do through water!

Opposite page:
King Penguins.

Home Sweet Home

When someone says the word *penguin* do you think of snowstorms and polar bears? If you do, you will be surprised to learn that these images are only partly true.

Penguins are only found in the southern hemisphere, that is the part of the world that lies south of the equator. Polars bears live in the Arctic, which is the northernmost part of the world. This means that penguins and polar bears are never seen together in the wild.

The shaded area on this map shows where penguins live.

The idea of a penguin being at home in the ice and snow is correct . . . at least for some species. But there are 18 different types of penguins, and some are found on the coasts of Australia, New Zealand, South Africa, Chile and Peru, and even on the Galapagos Islands at the equator!

6

Big Penguins, Little Penguins

When dinosaurs roamed the earth, the penguin's giant ancestor towered 1.5 metres (5 feet) tall. Now penguins are smaller. The largest is the Emperor Penguin, which may be the same height and weight as a ten-year-old. The smallest penguin is the Little or Fairy Penguin of Australia, which is only 35 centimetres (14 inches) tall and weighs 1 kilogram (2.2 pounds).

The smaller penguins are found closer to the equator. The biggest penguins—the Emperor, King, Adelie, Gentoo and Chinstrap—are found in the Antarctic. Their larger bodies keep warmer longer than the bodies of their smaller cousins. And keeping warm is important in the Antarctic!

8

Black and White

Did you ever wonder why penguins are black and white? As with many animals, the penguin's color pattern acts as camouflage and helps protect it from predators. Here's how it works. The dark back blends in with the dark waters of the ocean when viewed from above, making the penguin hard to spot by a predator looking down. On the other hand, if a hungry Killer Whale or Leopard Seal approaches from underneath, the white belly makes the penguin almost invisible against the sunny surface of the sea.

Of course, this black and white pattern is of little help on land, but adult penguins have few predators there. Killer Whales cannot follow them ashore, and seals and sea lions aren't fast enough to catch a penguin on land.

The Black-footed Penguin has an ideal coat for camouflage.

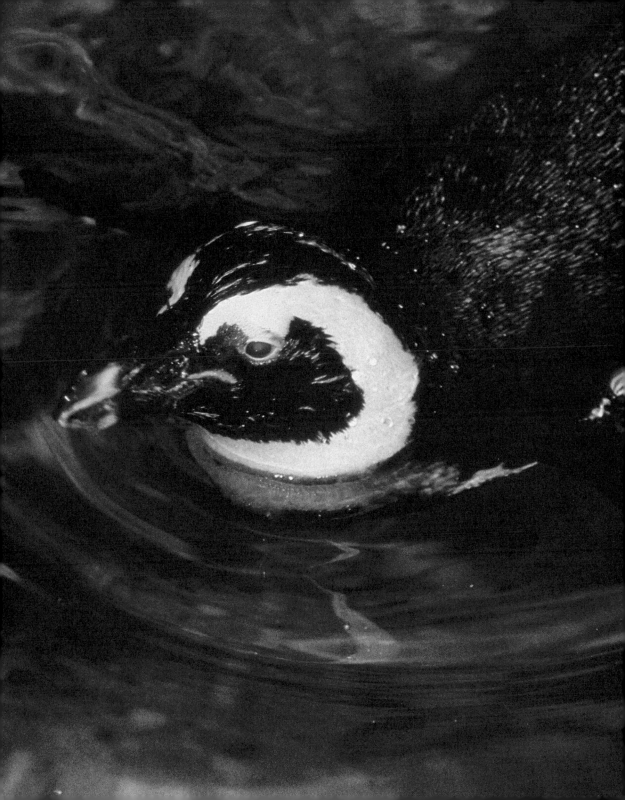

Penguin Patterns

We all know that penguins are black and white, but did you know that each species has a specific black and white color pattern?

Some penguins have black lines on their chests or necks while others have white spots on their heads. So it's easy to tell one type from another.

Moreover, most species of penguins aren't *just* black and white. Some have red or pink beaks while others have orange or red feet. A few have bright red or yellow eyes and some have patches of orange or yellow on their heads or chests. And there are even a few species that have tufts of bright feathers around their eyes that look like bushy eyebrows.

The Macaroni Penguin is unusual because of the long colorful feathers on its head.

Penguins on Parade

One of the penguin's most endearing features is its upright waddle across the ice with its wings spread out at its side. A penguin is not built quite like other birds, whose legs are near the center of their bodies. Instead, a penguin's legs are far back on its body near the tail. This causes it to walk upright, just like people.

The penguin uses its wings to balance on land but cannot lift them very high or fold them like other birds. This is because of the way the wing joint is built to help make swimming easier.

Waddling off into the sunset.

Diving Daredevils

Penguins spend more than two-thirds of their life swimming in the ocean. Their streamlined bodies, shaped like a submarine, move easily through the water, and they are expert swimmers. Pumping their stiff, flipper-like wings, they "fly" through the water, using their stubby tail and webbed feet as a rudder to steer.

Penguins are one of the top divers of animals that breathe air. Like the other champion divers, seals and whales, penguins are able to dive much deeper than humans. However, because penguins breathe air they cannot stay underwater too long.

Penguins can dive so well because they have solid bones. These bones give the birds added weight, which helps them to dive deep and to withstand the great pressure found underwater. Most other birds have hollow, lightweight bones, which are perfect for flying.

In some parts of the Antarctic Ocean penguins swim in water so cold that we would die if we took even a short dip.

Raincoats and Thermal Underwear

Penguins are birds and, like all birds, they have feathers. So how can they spend so much time frolicking in the ocean?

Penguin feathers are unique. They are very small, no longer than the bristles on your toothbrush. The tips are very stiff and they overlap like shingles to form a tight waterproof coat. This, and the natural oils from the penguin's skin, keep it dry.

Underneath the waterproof feathers is a thick coat of soft down right next to the bird's skin. This layer traps warm air near the penguin's body and keeps it snug against the cold winds and ocean waters. Some penguins even have a layer of fat, or blubber, under their skin for extra insulation. As well, tough pads on the bottom of the penguin's feet keep out the cold and stop them from freezing.

A pair of warmly dressed King Penguins.

A New Wardrobe

Each year, a penguin's feathers wear out and they must be replaced. New feathers under the skin begin to push through the old feathers. The old feathers fall out once the new ones have come in. This is called molting.

Molting takes a great deal of energy. During this time, which can last up to five weeks, a penguin may lose up to half its body weight! While molting the penguin must stay on land— because without its thick, protective coat to keep it warm and dry, it could not survive in the icy water.

Like all penguins King Penguins molt once a year.

A Seafood Feast

Even when penguins live as far north as the equator they will not swim in warm water. In fact, they will only enter the cold currents of the Antarctic Ocean, which flow throughout the southern hemisphere. These icy waters are particularly rich in the foods that penguins like best.

Penguins get all their food from the ocean but not all penguins eat the same things. The Macaroni Penguin—which got its name from the feathers behind its eyes which look like macaroni—feeds on squid and shrimp. The Peruvian Penguin prefers small fish, such as anchovies. While most penguins eat fish and shellfish, others also enjoy a large quantity of tiny, shrimp-like creatures called krill.

Penguins are big eaters. It is believed that they may eat more than half the food taken by predators in the southern oceans.

Adelie Penguins diving for a shrimp dinner.

Perfect Gentlemen?

Penguins may look like cute stuffed toys and perfect gentlemen in their ''tuxedos,'' but that soft, cuddly image is very misleading. Penguins are hunters and they are built to survive. They have razor-sharp beaks which are perfect for catching and eating their dinner swiftly and efficiently. Their small wings may not look like much, but they are capable of delivering a mightly blow if an intruder should get too close to their nest.

The beak of the Black-footed Penguin is strong and sharp.

Cooling Off

It may seem strange that penguins need to cool off. But, as you know, some penguins are found in warm climates, and on sunny summer days in the Antarctic the temperature rises above freezing. That might not seem hot to you, but for the Emperor Penguin it is mighty warm.

One of the easiest ways a penguin can cool off is probably a trick you have tried yourself: a quick dip into water.

Another thing adult penguins can do is fluff up their feathers and let as much air as possible circulate close to their skin. When they do this, you can see their bright pink skin.

Sometimes a penguin will hold its wings away from the sides of its body or flap them. These actions let more air come in contact with blood vessels on the underside of the wing. And that also helps to cool down the penguin.

"I think I'm a little overdressed for this weather!" (Emperor Penguin)

Bobsledding Home

Each year, after many months of hunting and feeding at sea, penguins return to their nesting grounds. For some, this may involve a simple hop onto the shore or a short walk to a nearby cave. But for others it is a long trek.

Emperor and Adelie penguins nest inland more than 100 kilometres (60 miles) from the Antarctic ice shelf. If you have ever seen a penguin waddling along, you might wonder how they manage to make this long trip.

Actually, in soft snow, a penguin can run as fast as a person. But to cover long distances and to conserve energy, penguins turn themselves into little self-propelled toboggans. By flopping onto their tummies and using their wings and feet for propulsion, they can cover great distances quite quickly. In spite of the cold ice next to their bodies, the penguins are kept warm by all the exercise. Sometimes they may even have to stop and fluff out their feathers to cool off!

Opposite page:
Some penguins must travel long distances by land or by sea to reach their nesting grounds. They use the sun to navigate.

Love Birds

Although it is difficult for us to tell a male penguin from a female, or to recognize a particular penguin in a huge rookery full of them, penguins have no such problem. They can tell each other apart, and year after year they return to the rookeries to find their previous mates. Often male penguins arrive at the rookery first and start squabbling over the best nesting sites. Once they have staked out their territory, they patiently wait for their mates to arrive.

When the happy pair is reunited there is quite a display. Greetings may include braying, croaking, trumpeting and cooing. They beat their flippers, clack their bills and dance. As you can imagine this is a very noisy, chaotic time in the rookery.

Foot Nests

Most penguins lay two eggs. But the female King and Emperor penguins lay only one egg and they do so in the middle of the Antarctic winter. Once the egg is laid, the father penguin takes over. Using his beak, he nudges the egg on top of his feet and wriggles until it lies safely tucked away under a special flap of belly skin. For the next two months, he is left to care for the egg. The father penguins huddle together against the bitterly cold winter, moving little and eating nothing.

During this time, the females return to the ocean to feed and store up fat before they return to care for their young chick.

Fancy footwork! (King Penguin)

Building a Nest

Although the King and Emperor penguins have their own built-in nests, other penguins must build a nest for their eggs. These penguins often nest in open areas where there are not a lot of materials to use, so they have to make do with whatever is handy.

Many penguins, including those that nest on the rocky coast of Antarctica, collect small pebbles. A pebble nest helps to keep the eggs off the cold ground and prevents them from getting wet if the snow melts quickly or there is a sudden rainstorm.

Other penguins use coarse grass, twigs, moss and even seaweed for their nests. Sometimes these penguins build their nests inside rock crevices or burrows. At other times they may dig into the sand or down into the excrement, or guano, that has been left by thousands of generations of penguins. These hollows act as extra shelter against bad weather and predators.

An Adelie Penguin returns to the nest to offer its mate a pebble.

Hatching

Penguin chicks may take up to three days to break out of their shell completely. When they finally pop through, they are moist from the egg sack. They dry quickly into fluffy, downy balls, usually brown in color.

Emperor Penguin chicks are the only ones born without a covering of down feathers. They are kept warm by their father. How? He has a naked patch under his belly flap where he has plucked off all the feathers. This little ''hot spot'' is called a brood patch and it allows more of the parent's body heat to reach the egg. Then when the chick is born, its naked body helps it to get the most heat from the parent's body while it stays snuggled under the built-in shelter.

Penguin chicks rely on their parents not only for food but also for warmth. They cannot control their own body temperature for 2 weeks.

Penguin Parents

Both penguin parents share the task of caring for their young. Since eggs and baby penguins are very vulnerable they must be protected. Also, penguin chicks need so much food in their first weeks of life that the job is simply too big for one parent.

Penguin parents split the duties. One stands guard while the other goes off to bring back food for the hungry chick or chicks. Some penguins take regular turns at the two tasks, while others simply divide them, based on the parent's sex. Before Royal and Rockhopper chicks are born, for instance, the female sits on the nest while the male goes off to feed and store up fat for his stint of chick sitting. After the chicks are born, the father stands guard while the hen goes off to get food.

When mother returns she is carrying almost half her body weight in partially digested food. The chicks place their beaks inside mom's mouth. She then brings the food back up into her mouth for them to eat.

Opposite page:
Keeping this Gentoo Penguin chick fed is a full time job.

Getting Bigger

Finally, the day comes when the chicks need more food than one parent can provide. The young are now left unguarded while both parents go off to collect food. For some male penguins it is finally a chance to start eating again. While collecting food for junior, of course. By this time the young have grown bigger and although they are not totally safe from hungry birds, such as skuas and sheathbills, they are capable of defending themselves.

This Black-footed Penguin chick will become black and white once its adult feathers grow in.

Penguin Daycare

Many kinds of penguins gather their young together into special nurseries, called crèches. Chicks move into the crèches as soon as they begin to walk, which may be anywhere from 10 to 45 days after they hatch.

Crèches are good for several reasons. Both parents can now find food knowing that their chick is not alone and, in cold climates, the chicks can huddle together for warmth. Also, the young are safer in a large group, because it is harder for hungry seabirds to choose a tasty morsel for dinner.

When a parent returns, it utters a few loud ''Supper!'' calls and the chick comes running. If another chick should happen by, it is ignored or even driven away by the parent.

A King and Gentoo crèche.

Swimming Lessons

Not all types of penguin chicks grow at the same rate. It takes Little Blue and Adelie penguins only two months to grow up while King Penguins take twelve to fourteen months. During this time their downy feathers are replaced by adult feathers. Penguin chicks cannot take to the water until they have this protective coat covering their body.

And then one day it happens. The penguin parents return to the rookery to feed their chick, only to find it is gone. The young one has decided it is time to head to the water to begin its ocean life. Without any lessons, the youngster plunges into the ocean and begins to swim.

To a penguin parent, the empty nest is a sign that their harried hunt to feed their chick is over. They too can return to the ocean.

Words To Know

Brood patch A featherless patch on the underside of a penguin's body that allows body heat to warm incubating eggs and newly hatched chicks.

Camouflage Colors and patterns that help an animal blend in with its surroundings.

Cock A male penguin.

Colony Large group of nesting birds.

Crèche Nursery group into which penguin chicks may be gathered for warmth and safety while the parents hunt for food.

Guano A bird's bodily wastes.

Hen A female penguin.

Krill Very small shrimp-like creatures that live in the ocean.

Mate To come together to produce young. Either member of an animal pair is also the other's mate.

Molting To shed one set of feathers.

Navigate To find the way from one place to another.

Predator An animal that hunts other animals for food.

Rookery A colony.

INDEX

Cover Photo: Kjell B. Sandved

Photo Credits: Kjell B. Sandved, pages 4, 8, 19, 20, 23, 27, 31, 35, 40; Y.J. Rey-Millett, World Wildlife Fund, page 7; Bill Ivy, pages 11, 24, 43; Ian Strange, World Wildlife Fund, page 12; L.G. Ziesler, Hot Shots, page 15; Masterfile, page 16; Paul Drummond, Canapress, pages 28, 36; D. Roby, Academy of Natural Sciences, page 37; Dr. A. Sutter, World Wildlife Fund, page 44.

Getting To Know...

Nature's Children

ELEPHANTS

Elin Kelsey

SCHOLASTIC INC.

New York   Toronto   London   Auckland   Sydney
Mexico City   New Delhi   Hong Kong   Buenos Aires

Facts in Brief

Classification of the elephant

      Class: *Mammalia* (mammals)

      Order: *Proboscidea* (animals with proboscises)

      Family: *Elephantidae* (elephant family)

      Genus: *Loxodonta* and *Elephas*

      Species: *Loxodonta africana* (African elephant); *Elephas maximus* (Asian and Indian elephant)

World distribution. Asia and Africa.

Habitat. Forest, plains and marshes.

Distinctive physical characteristics. Loose-fitting gray skin, long prehensile trunk; both male and female African elephants have tusks, usually only male Asian elephants have tusks.

Habits. Females and young live together in small herds, males live alone or in small all-male groups. Elephants forage constantly in order to get enough to eat and so must keep moving around.

Published by Scholastic Inc.
90 Old Sherman Turnpike, Danbury, Connecticut 06816.

SCHOLASTIC and associated logos are trademarks of Scholastic Inc.

ISBN 0-7172-6687-7

Printed in the U.S.A.

Have you ever wondered . . .

The last time you went to a movie they were probably selling jumbo-sized drinks, bags of popcorn and candy bars. Did you ever stop to wonder how the word "jumbo" came to mean extra large?

Jumbo was the name of a very famous elephant. He was one of the first elephants to appear in an American circus. Everyone who met Jumbo was fascinated by his incredible size and fell in love with his gentle and charming personality. To know Jumbo was to love him. Although Jumbo was in many ways unique, elephants *are* very special animals. Read on to find out why.

The elephant is our largest land animal.

Elephant I.D.

Although some elephants come from Africa and others from Asia, you can recognize any elephant by its huge body and wrinkled trunk.

The easiest way to tell where an elephant comes from is to look at its ears. An African elephant's ears are truly enormous. In fact, they are nearly twice as large as the ears of an Asian elephant.

The shape of an elephant's body also provides important clues. Asian elephants' high, round heads and arched backs give them a chubby appearance. African elephants have low, rather flat foreheads and their backs are slightly U-shaped. Also, the head of an African elephant hangs below its shoulders, while the Asian elephant holds its head higher.

Can you tell what kind of elephants these are?

6

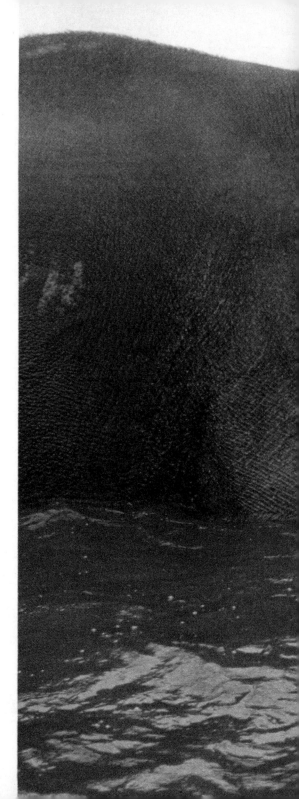

Elephant-Land

Elephants live in tropical countries where it is warm all year round. For most of the year the weather is hot and dry. But during the rainy season it is very wet.

Most African elephants live south of the Sahara Desert in open grassy areas called savannas. However, with the exception of the desert areas, elephants have been found in every kind of African environment, including rocky mountain slopes. Asian elephants are found in India, Sri Lanka, South China and Southeast Asia. They live mainly in forested areas.

Opposite page: *The elephant's pillar-like legs are designed to support its great weight.*

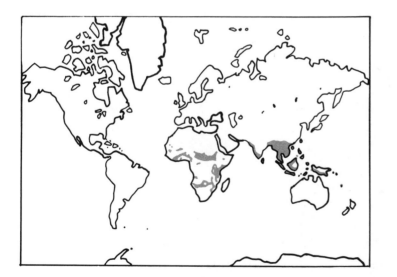

The shaded area on this map shows where elephants live.

African elephant.

Asian elephant.

Jumbo Sized

If elephants played basketball they would have a distinct advantage. A full-grown male African elephant is so tall he could look *down* into the basketball net! An Asian male elephant would have to be careful, though. He's just the right height to bump his head on the hoop.

Not only are elephants tall, they are also very heavy. A male African elephant can weigh up to 6000 kilograms (13,000 pounds), which is about five or six times as much as your family car! The lighter Asian male averages about 4500 (10,000 pounds).

Female elephants are usually smaller than the males and weigh quite a bit less.

The only hair on an elephant's body is at the tip of its tail, which serves as a handy fly swatter.

Gigantic Appetites

An elephant's enormous size is matched by its gigantic appetite. If you were to invite an elephant over for salad, it could eat more than 900 platefuls! And it needs almost a bathtub full of water a day to wash it all down!

An elephant needs so much food that it usually spends at least 16 hours a day eating. This means that by the time it reaches its sixtieth birthday, an elephant may have spent 40 years of its life eating!

Elephants will eat a wide variety of plants and fruit but they do have particular favorites. African elephants love grass—up to 90 percent of their diet is grass. They also snack on tree bark and fruit. Asian elephants feed mainly on leaves, plant roots, flowers and bamboo.

An elephant uses its tusks to strip tasty bark off a tree.

Teeth

If you've ever munched on a stringy piece of celery, you'll have some idea of what elephant food is like. It needs a lot of chewing before it can be swallowed. Elephants are well equipped to chew up all this tough food. Here's how.

Throughout your life, you will have two sets of teeth—your baby and then your adult teeth. Elephants, on the other hand, have six sets of teeth!

Only four of an elephant's gigantic brick-shaped teeth, called molars, are in use at any one time. These molars can be found one on each side of the upper and lower jaw. They first come in at the back of the jaw and slowly move forward as they are needed. In other words, when the tooth in the front is worn down and falls out, there's another one ready to take its place.

Because it has such a short neck, the elephant can't reach the ground with its mouth, so it must rely on its trunk to pick up food.

14

Trusty Tusks

An elephant's tusks are actually huge, pointed, ivory teeth that keep on growing throughout the elephant's life. Both male and female African elephants have long white tusks. In some large males, each tusk may weigh as much as your mom or dad. Male Asian elephants have smaller tusks, and often the females do not have tusks at all.

Elephants put their tusks to many different uses. They use them to dig for roots and to peel the bark off trees. When water is scarce they drill for water in dry river beds with their tusks. Occasionally they will even use them as weapons. And when things are peaceful, tusks make a great trunk rest.

Overleaf:
When an elephant and rhino meet they usually go about their own business.

Only two-thirds of an elephant's tusk is visible, the rest is embedded in the skull.

Wondrous Trunks

Have you ever played "push the penny" with your nose? It isn't easy. Your nose is so small that it is difficult to make it do much more than breathe, smell and occasionally wiggle. But an elephant's nose is something else again!

An elephant's nose together with its upper lip form a flexible trunk that can be used for just about everything. Imagine being able to scratch, lift, carry, throw, touch, smell, shower and hug —all using your nose!

The end of the trunk is as sensitive as your fingertips. With it, an elephant can pick up a single blade of grass. An elephant's trunk contains more than 40,000 muscles and tendons, which make it very strong and flexible. That's why elephants can also use their trunks to lift heavy logs or to push down tasty-looking trees.

One of the most important uses for a trunk, however, is to smell. By sticking its trunk in the air an elephant can keep aware of danger. It can also smell ripe fruit as far as four city blocks away! Yum.

Opposite page:
The tip of the Asian elephant's trunk has one small fleshy "finger," unlike that of the African elephant which has two.

20

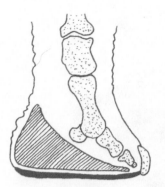

X-ray of an elephant's foot.

Opposite page:
An elephant convoy.

Elephants on the Move

An elephant needs so much food and water that it may have to travel great distances to find enough. Most of the time an elephant strolls along at about the same speed as you jog. Should something startle it, however, it can race away at 40 kilometres (25 miles) an hour.

Would you believe that an elephant can move around almost silently when it wants to? It's true. Although elephants have enormous feet —some are bigger than serving platters—they are not loud and clumsy. In fact, the special design of their feet allows them to walk quietly and gracefully.

If you saw an X-ray of an elephant's foot, you would notice that the toe bones are permanently pointed on tiptoe. A fatty, elastic pad beneath the toes and heel forms a spongy cushion that enables the elephant to walk almost silently, leaving hardly any tracks. Ridges on the sole of an elephant's foot help it to get a good grip on rocky slopes or when climbing out of slippery mud holes.

Elephant Roads

Elephants travel on special trails. Many of these were first made hundreds of years earlier by the elephant's great-great-great-grandparents. Each trail leads to a favorite feeding area or watering hole.

Traveling elephants move in an orderly single file. As if marching in a parade, each one carefully places its feet one in front of the other. Elephants step so carefully that their trails remain very narrow— just wide enough for them to squeeze through.

Elephant mothers make sure their youngsters stay very near them on the trail. A baby elephant will walk between its mother's front legs. When it gets a little older it will hang on to her tail, now and then receiving a helpful pull if the path becomes steep or slippery.

24

Keeping Cool

If you want to find an elephant at noon on a sweltering hot day, start by looking under a tall tree. Whenever it can, that's where an elephant will go spend the midday hours resting in the shade to avoid overheating. And if it gets really hot, an elephant has a very special way of cooling down: it waves its ears!

An elephant's ears are full of blood vessels. By flapping its ears, an elephant cools down the blood that circulates through them. The cooled blood is then pumped back through the elephant, lowering the temperature of its entire body.

African elephants have larger ears than the forest-dwelling Asian elephants. That is because African elephants live in open grassy areas where they can't always find shade. They need larger ears to help them keep cool. Each of an African elephant's enormous ears weighs about twice as much as you do!

"I'm all ears!"

Mud Baths

Most of us like to take bubble baths. Elephants like to bathe too, but instead of bubble baths they take mud baths! Skidding, rolling and splashing, a group of elephants will wallow in a gooey mud hole until they are covered from trunk to toe.

It looks like great fun and it probably is, but it serves a useful purpose too. The skin of an elephant looks tough and leathery, but it is actually very sensitive. A nice thick coat of mud goes a long way towards protecting it from the hot, drying sun and irritating insect bites. And just in case that is not sufficient, an elephant will often follow its bath with a powdering of dust for extra bug protection!

An elephant takes a dust bath by sucking dirt up its trunk and blowing it out over itself.

Everybody in the Pool

Elephants head for water whenever they get the chance. They enjoy playing in water and they also drink enormous quantities of it. They do not suck it up through their trunks as some people think. They use their trunks to hold the water before squirting it into their mouths. They also shower their backs with water to cool themselves.

Believe it or not, these gigantic animals are excellent swimmers! They often swim underwater with only their trunks and the tips of their ears above the surface. An elephant's trunk functions like a diver's snorkel. With its trunk held up, an elephant can swim underwater for hours and travel great distances.

"Come on in, the water's fine!"

30

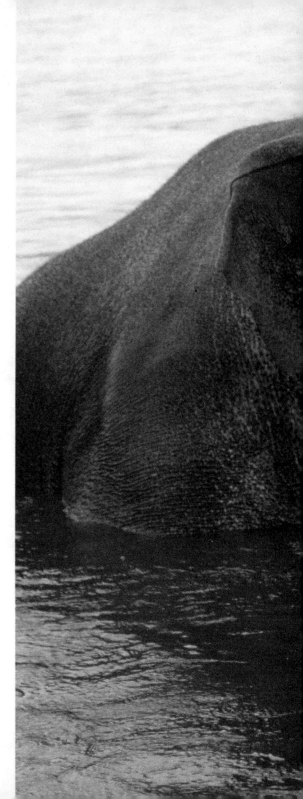

The Right Moves

Elephants have special ways of communicating. Just as your facial expression reflects your mood, the position of an elephant's head, ears, tail and trunk show how the elephant is feeling.

Friends often shake hands or hug when they meet each other. How do elephant friends say hello? They like to sniff each other and drape their trunks over one another's backs or wrap their trunks together.

A curious elephant will cock its ears forward and lift its trunk high in the air. If it smells something exciting it will flap its ears back and forth. If it senses danger it will spread its ears out and rap on the ground with its trunk as a warning.

Elephant Talk

As well as body language elephants use sounds to communicate. And since they are very sociable animals they make a lot of different sounds depending on what's happening.

The best-known elephant sound is trumpeting. This noise comes through the trunk to make it extra loud. It means that an elephant is excited, surprised, ready to attack or has become separated from the herd.

If an elephant is feeling contented, it will hang its trunk down straight and produce a rumbling sound deep in its throat. The happy elephant is purring! Since elephants purr more often in areas where there are lots of trees and they can't see one another, scientists think it is the elephants' way of keeping track of one another.

Usually elephants make sounds that can be heard quite clearly. Scientists have recently discovered, however, that sometimes the noises may be so low that only other elephants can hear them. This may help them to "talk" over long distances.

Opposite page:
Sounding the trumpet.

35

Living Together

Normally elephants live in small family groups called herds. A herd may contain as many as fifty elephants but smaller groups are more common. The surprising thing about an elephant herd is that only female elephants and their children belong to it. Adult male elephants or bulls live alone or in very small groups.

The oldest and wisest female elephant in the herd is the leader. Since elephants can live to be more than sixty years old, a leader may be very experienced. It is her job to protect the herd from danger. Because she knows where to find the best watering holes and feeding areas, she decides where the group will travel.

Members of an elephant herd are extremely close. If one elephant is injured or ill, the others will nurse it back to health. If an elephant has difficulty walking, two elephants will use their strong bodies to support the injured animal from either side.

Asian elephants spend the hottest times of the day in shady woods.

A Baby is Born

If you have ever had to wait for a new baby in your family you know that nine months can be an awfully long time. But imagine this: elephant mothers are pregnant for almost two years!

Elephants don't have doctors to deliver their babies but they do receive lots of help. As the time of birth draws closer, the mother becomes the center of attention. The other female elephants stay close by her side. When the exciting moment arrives, they are there to help and they won't leave until the new baby is up on its feet.

The members of the herd keep a careful watch to make sure that nothing harms the baby. Since it is too weak to travel during the first few days of its life, the herd won't set out on the trail until the newcomer can keep up.

It takes a baby elephant about 6 months to learn how to use its trunk properly.

Big Babies

Elephants have big babies. A new baby elephant is about as tall as a three-year-old child and weighs 100 kilograms (220 pounds) or more. It is called a calf.

The first thing the hairy calf does is wobble to its feet in search of milk. It has a big appetite and drinks about 10 litres (40 cups) of milk every day. (In case you wondered, a baby elephant, like all baby mammals, nurses with its mouth, not its trunk.)

Although the young elephant may start eating plants in its second year, it will continue to drink its mother's milk until it is three or four years old. It grows quickly and by the age of six it will probably weigh ten times as much as when it was born.

Lunchtime!

Staying Safe

Because they are so big and powerful, adult elephants have no natural enemies. Baby elephants, however, sometimes need protection from the lions of the African plains or Asia's tigers. At the first sign of danger, the adult members of a herd will form a tight circle with all of the younger elephants in the center. Then the adults will trumpet loudly and thrust their ears out to the side, like enormous pairs of wings. Sometimes these outstretched ears make the elephant appear so much bigger, the enemy may turn and run away. Should the intruder linger too long, the largest elephants will press their ears tightly against their heads and charge!

Elephant cows are very attentive mothers and won't let any intruders near their young.

Growing Up

Young elephants are very playful. By the time they are a year old, they love to wrestle and tumble in the mud, poking each other with their trunks and squealing with delight.

The youngsters learn by exploring and by imitating the other members of the herd. An elephant mother is very loving and offers lots of encouragement. However, she is firm about good behavior. Should a calf throw a tantrum, a quick trunk slap usually settles things down.

An elephant continues to grow all its life, though much more slowly in later years. It will, however, be considered grown *up* at ten or so. At about that age, the male elephants leave the herd and travel alone or in small groups. The females stay with their mothers, aunts and grandmothers and soon begin raising families of their own.

Words To Know

Bull A male elephant.

Calf A young elephant.

Cow A female elephant.

Herd A group of animals traveling and feeding together.

Molars Large blunt teeth that are used to grind food.

Nurse To drink milk from a mother's body.

Savanna A grassy plain.

Snorkel A breathing tube used by divers.

Tendon A tough band of tissue that attaches a muscle to a bone or some other part.

Trunk The long flexible snout of an elephant formed with the upper lip and the nose with the nostrils at the end.

Tusks Special teeth that grow down out of the mouths of some animals such as elephants.

INDEX

Cover Photo: Art Gryfe, Network Stock Photo File

Photo Credits: Bob Wavra, page 4; Bill Ivy, pages 7, 21, 31; Chris Harvey, Masterfile, page 8; Robert Winslow, pages 11, 15, 25; William Smyth, page 12; Jack Templeton, page 16; Bradley Smith, Animals Animals, pages 18-19; Victor Burville, The Stock Market, page 23; B. Littlejohn, The Stock Market, page 26; John Rushmer, Hot Shots, pages 29, 33; Harvey Medland, Network Stock Photo, page 34; R. Homewood, page 37; Tony Stone Worldwide, Masterfile, page 39; Tony Stone Worldwide, The Stock Market, pages 40-41; Lori Labatt, Hot Shots, page 43; Boyd Norton, page 45.